Our
Guest
Book